A WORLD IN DANGER

WINDIER

BY
BRENDA MCHALE

PowerKiDS
press™

New York

Published in 2022 by The Rosen
Publishing Group, Inc.
29 East 21st Street, New York, NY 10010

© 2022 Booklife Publishing
This edition is published by arrangement
with Booklife Publishing

Edited by:
Madeline Tyler

Designed by:
Gareth Liddington

Cataloging-in-Publication Data

Names: McHale, Brenda.
Title: Windier / Brenda McHale.
Description: New York : PowerKids Press,
2022. | Series: A world in danger |
Includes glossary and index.
Identifiers: ISBN 9781725336094 (pbk.) |
ISBN 9781725336117 (library bound) |
ISBN 9781725336100 (6 pack) |
ISBN 9781725336124 (ebook)
Subjects: LCSH: Climatic changes--Juvenile
literature. | Storms--Juvenile literature. |
Natural disasters--Juvenile literature.
Classification: LCC QC903.15 M343 2022 |
DDC 551.55'4--dc23

Manufactured in the United States
of America

CPSIA Compliance Information: Batch #CWPK22.
For Further Information contact Rosen Publishing,
New York, New York at 1-800-237-9932.

Find us on

PHOTO CREDITS

Cover & Throughout – Minerva Studio, Kivi Design, Sloth Astronaut, solarseven, Sergey Nivens, 2&3 – Rasica, solarseven, 4&5 – Creative Travel Projects,
Aleksei Chugunov, 6&7 – Sepp photography, Rudmer Zwerver, 8&9 – Kichigin, trgrowth, 10&11 – andreiuc88, Tiina Tuomaala, Lester Balajadia, 12&13 –
elRoce, AMFPhotography, 14&15 – David Burkholder, Tim Roberts Photography, Mfield, 16&17 – Jonathan Berry, StevenKingArt, 18&19 – GLF Media, Anne
Powell, 20&21 – Cameron Ballantyne-Smith, think4photop, 22&23 – Kodda, David Tadevosian, Africa Studio.

Images are courtesy of Shutterstock.com. With thanks to Getty Images, Thinkstock Photo and iStockphoto.

All facts, statistics, web addresses and URLs in this book were verified as valid and accurate at time of writing.
No responsibility for any changes to external websites or references can be accepted by either the author or publisher.

CONTENTS

Words that look like <u>this</u> can be found in the glossary on page 24.

ARE WEATHER AND CLIMATE DIFFERENT?

Sunny, stormy, snowy, and windy are all types of weather.

Weather is what happens day to day. Weather changes a lot. When the weather is similar for a while, it is called a <u>season</u>. There is usually cold weather in winter and warm weather in summer.

Climate is what the weather is like over a very long time. When we talk about a hot place or a cold place, we are talking about climate. There are different kinds of climate.

Some climates are hot and <u>humid</u>.

WHAT IS CLIMATE CHANGE?

The <u>global</u> climate is changing. Different areas of the world are getting hotter, drier, windier, or wetter. This is called climate change, and it affects all sorts of weather.

We need to stop harming our planet because it's the only one we have!

The climate changes all the time, but usually it is natural and happens very slowly. Now, it is being caused by the way people are living and is happening much faster.

WHY IS EARTH GETTING WARMER?

We burn <u>fossil fuels</u> to make electricity, to power our cars, and to keep our houses warm. Burning fossil fuels makes harmful <u>gases</u> called greenhouse gases.

Usually, a lot of the sun's heat bounces off Earth's surface and back into space through the <u>atmosphere</u>. Greenhouse gases in the atmosphere trap heat on Earth, making it warmer.

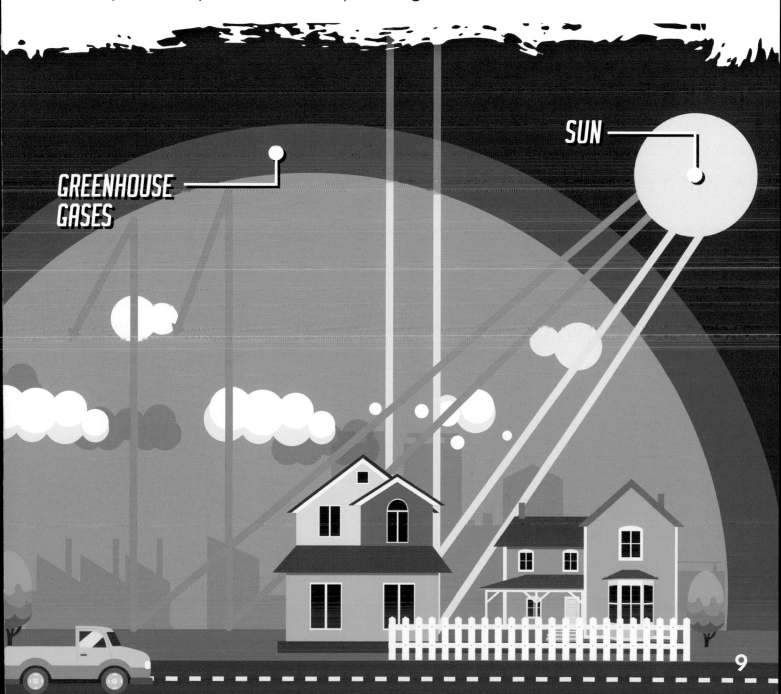

GREENHOUSE GASES

SUN

WHY IS IT WINDIER?

When air warms, it rises. Cooler air rushes in to take its place. That moving air is the wind. Climate change makes more warm air. This means more air is moving, so there is more wind.

WARM AIR RISING

COLD AIR RUSHING IN

Some winds are made by changes in a small area of the world. Global winds are made by Earth spinning and the difference in temperature between the <u>poles</u> and the <u>equator</u>.

WHAT IS A HURRICANE?

EYE

It is usually calm in the eye of a hurricane.

A hurricane is a huge storm with very fast winds that move in a circle. There is rain in a hurricane because warm air holds more <u>moisture</u> than cold air. Hurricanes form over warm seas and are strongest over water.

Hurricanes cause massive waves called storm surges that flood big areas. Hurricanes destroy buildings and harm people and animals. They can damage plants being grown for food.

Hurricanes are also called cyclones or typhoons.

HURRICANE KATRINA

Hurricane Katrina hit the coast of the United States in August 2005. There was a storm surge that broke down the walls built to stop flooding. Most of the city of New Orleans, Louisiana, flooded.

People were killed by damaged buildings and flooding. Most people had to move out of the city and many never moved back. It cost a lot of money to rebuild and fix all the damage.

AUSTRALIAN DUST STORM

Some people said it looked like Mars!

In 2009, there was a very big dust storm in Australia. The air was so full of dust it was hard to see. The red dust was soil from dry areas of Australia, carried by strong winds.

TORNADOES

Tornadoes are spinning towers of wind that move very fast and cause damage. When dust gets trapped in a spinning tornado it is called a dust devil.

Tornadoes are sometimes called twisters. They're common in the United States.

DO STRONGER WINDS MATTER?

Countries need to make sure buildings and homes can stand up to strong winds. People may have to leave their homes if they live where tornadoes, hurricanes, and storm surges are common.

This storm surge <u>barrier</u> is in the Netherlands. The gates can close to protect the nearby city.

GATES

Can you see the birds chasing the boat to catch anything that is missed?

NETS TO CATCH THE FISH

Winds change sea <u>currents</u> by blowing the water. The changing sea currents change where fish gather. It also affects boats traveling around the world.

IS IT TOO LATE TO SLOW CLIMATE CHANGE?

Climate change is happening, but scientists think we can slow it down. Lots of people go to <u>protests</u> to tell leaders that they must make new laws to save Earth.

People all over the world can do something to help. If everyone does something small, it can make a big difference.

Can you be a climate superhero?

HOW CAN WE HELP?

People need to produce fewer greenhouse gases. That means using less energy and fuel. Walking or riding your bike instead of taking the car somewhere is one way to cut down on using fuel.

Power plants use fossil fuels to make electricity.

Making new things often releases greenhouse gases. Instead of throwing old things away, you could try reusing and recycling.

Use your imagination with old bottles and boxes.

To change clothes, give them new life by using fabric pens. Always check with a grown-up first.

GLOSSARY

atmosphere   the mixture of gases that make up the air and surround Earth

barrier   something that blocks the way

currents   movements or flows of water or air in one direction

equator   the imaginary line around Earth that is an equal distance from the North and South Poles

fossil fuels   fuels, such as coal, oil, and gas, that formed millions of years ago from the remains of animals and plants

gases   matter, like air, which fills any space available

global   relating to the whole world

humid   air containing a high level of water; damp

moisture   a small amount of liquid, such as water, that makes something wet or moist

poles   the top and bottom points of Earth

protests   events where large groups of people show their dislike of a certain thing together

season   a certain part of the year—such as spring, summer, fall, or winter—that has similar weather throughout

INDEX